Acknowledgments:

I would like to acknowledge my teachers: Richard Schwartz, Philip Manfield, Janina Fisher, Bessel van der Kolk, Patricia Papernow, and Chris Burris. I also wish to thank my insightful and hardworking students, and especially my lionhearted clients, who are my most profound teachers in every way.

Illustrations by Steven Gong
Cover by Steven Gong & Amy Rubenzer
Layout by Steven Gong, Jen Wilson-Gaetz, and Amy Rubenzer
ISBN: 9781683734161
Printed in Canada

PESI Publishing
pesipublishing.com

We all have

Parts

AN ILLUSTRATED GUIDE TO HEALING TRAUMA WITH INTERNAL FAMILY SYSTEMS

COLLEEN WEST

LICENSED MARRIAGE & FAMILY THERAPIST

A Note From the Author

This book is a response to the many clients who have sought therapy for relief from their complex, painful, and confusing symptoms, only to leave disappointed because talking about their traumatic pasts seemed to make their symptoms worse. We know so much about treating trauma survivors, yet so many go without effective treatment. This is my attempt to make this complex subject more understandable and digestible, both for therapists and for those they serve. Learning about the effects of severe trauma and neglect, employing methods to reduce autonomic dysregulation, and beginning to befriend one's parts are strategies that are frequently liberating for even the most discouraged clients. When I started to work with my own traumatized parts, I wanted a book with lots of pictures—so I decided to create one! My dearest wish is that it helps you (or your clients) heal.

You are no longer alone.

The methods here are proven, though the work is neither easy nor fast. If you are a trauma survivor reading this, you are no longer alone, for in these words are love and boundless compassion, just leaping off the page, for you and all your parts.

Contents

Symptoms of Trauma Checklist   7

Window of Tolerance   8

Autonomic (Automatic) Defenses   12

But My Family Was Okay!   16

How We Learn to Protect   18

"Tracking" or "Mapping" Your Parts   22

Getting to Know & Care for Your Parts   24

Getting to Know Protectors   26

Getting to Know Exiles   28

Inner Critics   30

Self-Energy   32

All Parts Welcome   34

First Aid for Triggered Parts   36

References   39

Trauma.

For our purposes, trauma is an injury—physical, sexual, or emotional—so severe that it shifts your fundamental reality, your ability to trust people, and your worldview. It can be either a single event or a long-standing pattern of injury, as with childhood abuse or neglect.

We know from studies there are many symptoms that result from psychological trauma. *Which ones do you relate to?*

Symptoms of Trauma Checklist

History of:

- ☐ Attachment failure
- ☐ Childhood neglect
- ☐ Community violence
- ☐ Criminal violence
- ☐ Discrimination
- ☐ Divorce
- ☐ Violent, frightening caregivers
- ☐ Early loss (death of caretaker, adoption)
- ☐ Family separation
- ☐ Hate crime
- ☐ Medical trauma
- ☐ Physical abuse
- ☐ Racism
- ☐ Sexual abuse

Emotional Symptoms:

- ☐ Anger/aggression
- ☐ Anxiety/panic attacks
- ☐ Inability to relax
- ☐ Chronic loneliness/isolation
- ☐ Constant self-criticism
- ☐ Depression
- ☐ Overwhelming emotions
- ☐ Fears/phobias
- ☐ Mood shifts/irritability
- ☐ Hopelessness
- ☐ Night terrors/nightmares
- ☐ Numbness/detachment
- ☐ Feeling overwhelmed
- ☐ Painful indecision
- ☐ Unresolved grief
- ☐ Difficulty being alone
- ☐ Difficulty feeling close to others
- ☐ Difficulty making/keeping friends
- ☐ Difficulty saying no
- ☐ Frequent conflict with others

Behavioral Symptoms:

- ☐ Addiction
- ☐ Lack of motivation
- ☐ Inability to slow down
- ☐ Eating disorder
- ☐ Impulsiveness/manic symptoms
- ☐ Inability to manifest
- ☐ Self-harm
- ☐ Sexual difficulties
- ☐ Social anxiety
- ☐ Social isolation
- ☐ Thoughts of suicide
- ☐ Underemployment

Cognitive Symptoms:

- ☐ Inability to make decisions
- ☐ Constant self-criticism
- ☐ Difficulty concentrating
- ☐ Frequent confusion
- ☐ Memory problems
- ☐ Negative/anxious rumination
- ☐ Negative beliefs about self

Somatic/Physical Symptoms:

- ☐ Autoimmune disease
- ☐ Chronic back pain
- ☐ Chronic exhaustion/fatigue
- ☐ Headaches
- ☐ Insomnia
- ☐ Irritable bowel syndrome
- ☐ Lack of appetite
- ☐ Unexplained physical symptoms

Sensory Symptoms:

- ☐ Hallucinations: visual, auditory, sensory, olfactory
- ☐ Lost time (inability to account for hour/day/week/year)
- ☐ Parts of the body feel unreal
- ☐ World feels unreal

West & Walker, 2018

Window of Tolerance

Emotions go up and down. When we can think clearly and feel our feelings at the same time, we are in the window of tolerance. Within the window of tolerance, we are our wisest and truest selves. In Buddhism, we would call this Buddha nature; in Christianity, the Soul. In this book, we call this wise-mind-peaceful-heart state the *Self,* with a capital S.

In hyper-arousal we are above the window—overstimulated.
In hypo-arousal we are below the window—shut down.

Trauma survivors spend too much time above and below the window of tolerance.

How do you know when you are above your window?
How do you know when you are below your window?

West & Walker, 2018

Sympathetic Nervous System

Parasympathetic Nervous system

HELP!

Hyper-Arousal

Feel an urgency to act, overstimulated, unsafe, hypervigilant, panicked, terrified, rageful, ruminative, overwhelmed, difficulty with sleep, loss of appetite

Window of Tolerance

Feelings are "right-sized," you can think clearly and feel your feelings at the same time, and you experience qualities of the Self, including calm, curiosity, clear thinking, connection to yourself and others, compassion, confidence, and courage

Hypo-Arousal

Feel numb, shut down, chronically exhausted, disconnected, disengaged, ashamed, deadened, depressed, may sleep too much, impulse to soothe with food

numb

Did you know your symptoms stem from implicit memories?

Trauma memories get stored as patterns held in the mind and body that were either formed in childhood or at the moment a particular trauma took place. Thoughts, images, emotions, and body sensations can all be memories. We know that memories exist in chains, often linked by a theme, like shame, terror, powerlessness, or abandonment. When all the memories in a chain open at once, the result is a flood of sensation.

Because the brain's emergency response system (the amygdala) is not oriented to time, but rather to immediate survival, it can feel as if no time has passed since the original traumatic event occurred. Thinking becomes hijacked. This happens frequently for trauma survivors and can range from mild discomfort to complete overwhelm. We call these "flashbacks."

The simple statements "This is a flashback," or "I feel afraid, but I am not in danger," or "This flashback will pass, as they always do" can bring your innate resource of perspective back online. Re-engaging the thinking/noticing brain (your prefrontal cortex) when you have been triggered into a flashback is a critical skill for you to practice many times, until you and your brain know how.

Trauma memories exist in chains.
Overwhelm happens when a whole chain opens at once.

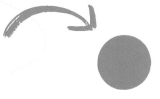

Fisher, 2016; Shapiro, 1995; Walker 2014; West & Walker, 2018

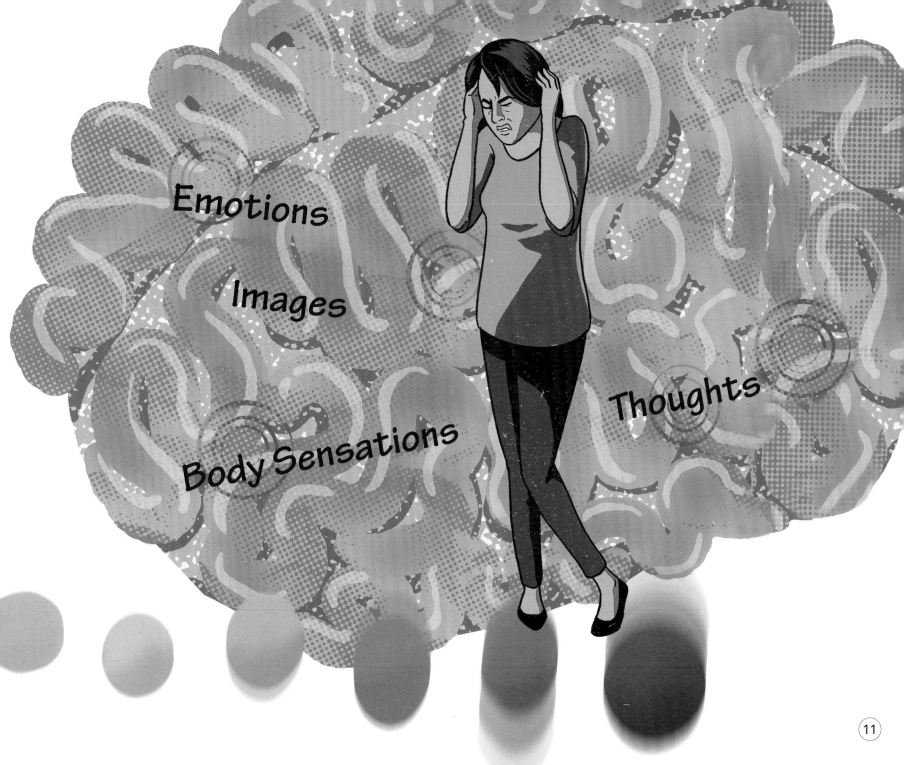

Autonomic (Automatic) Defenses

Under threat, your body is wired to protect you. Your physical and psychic survival depend on autonomic defenses. When you are triggered into one of these states, you might feel like a monster has taken over your mind and body because these are powerful, whole-body neurobiological reactions. The first part of healing your traumatized self is to learn to recognize these states when they happen.

Attach

Fight

Freeze

Flight

Submit

van der Hart, Nijenhuis, & Steele, 2006

Attach

- [ ] Crying out for help
- [ ] Longing
- [ ] Waiting by the phone
- [ ] Clinging
- [ ] Neediness
- [ ] Loneliness
- [ ] "Talk to me!"
- [ ] Terror of being abandoned

Submit

- [ ] Shame
- [ ] Trouble saying no
- [ ] Passive
- [ ] Self-critical
- [ ] Subjugated
- [ ] Compliant
- [ ] People pleasing
- [ ] Feeling worthless or "bad"
- [ ] Self-denial/self-sacrificing
- [ ] Caretaking of others

Freeze

- [ ] Terrified
- [ ] Panic attacks
- [ ] Unable to think/act
- [ ] No voice
- [ ] Guarded
- [ ] Frozen
- [ ] Heart racing
- [ ] Social anxiety

Flight

- [ ] Escape
- [ ] Fantasizing
- [ ] Eating disorders
- [ ] Numbing
- [ ] Binge watching
- [ ] Chronic worry
- [ ] Addictions
- [ ] Compulsions
- [ ] Spacey/foggy
- [ ] Smartphone checking

Fight

- [ ] Hypervigilant
- [ ] Explosive
- [ ] Judgmental
- [ ] Mistrustful
- [ ] Suicidal
- [ ] Controlling
- [ ] Hostile
- [ ] Rigid
- [ ] Self-destructive

As trauma survivors spend more and more time in a triggered state in order to survive, either physically or emotionally, many find they have one or two autonomic defenses that they fall into frequently.

Which of these do you relate to most?

Fisher, 2009; West & Walker, 2018

What did you learn from early caregivers about being close?

Caretakers who are...
- Punishing
- Violent
- Derisive
- Critical
- Interfering
- Intrusive
- Cold
- Exhibit hostile control

Caretakers who are...
- Absent
- Unreliable
- Self-centered
- Addictive
- Neglectful
- Make and break promises

Caretakers who are...
- Overprotective
- Too disclosing
- Emotionally enmeshed
- Overinvolved
- Have poor boundaries
- Exhibit anxious control

Caretakers who are...
- Alternately frightened and frightening
- Intermittently non-responsive and overreactive
- Alternately functional/non-functional
- Internally preoccupied

West & Walker, 2018

When early attachments are unsafe, confusing, icky, or cold, the human drive to be close gets wired with the need to be safe and to survive: two human drives in conflict. Under these circumstances, a child's ability to accurately read other peoples' faces, body language, and tone of voice is also compromised. This means any relationship can become confusing, painful, and problematic. Over time, many trauma survivors find intimate relationships just too difficult and may isolate from other people, even though they long for connection. *Some examples:*

Submission   Judgment

Desire   Coldness

Longing   Flight

van der Kolk, 2014; West & Walker, 2018

But my family was okay!

This is where the story of trauma becomes more subtle. Sometimes a family looks fine on the surface, but underneath people are suffering. Hidden trauma carried in the body of a well-intentioned parent can still be passed on to a child. For example, a parent who works, exercises, or worries compulsively may look great to outsiders, but they can do quiet harm to young, vulnerable psyches.

Other people have solidly caring parents, but even the best-intentioned parents cannot shield their children from everything! If you fall into either of these categories, it can be confusing to experience negative patterns and powerful feelings—even flashbacks—that are hard to explain.

It's hard to grow up.

Anyone who has been a child or adolescent knows how painful it can be to negotiate relationships with siblings, peers, and grown-ups, even if they mean well. Suffering—from illness, accidents, or loss of loved ones due to death or separation—is an unavoidable part of life. The result: carried pain, more time outside the window of tolerance through flashbacks, and an increased need to protect oneself.

Legacy burdens.

Every family carries some very painful experiences from past generations. Sometimes the story is so old that it is no longer being told, and yet it is affecting everyone. Histories of war, genocide, slavery, religious persecution, starvation, and poverty can all affect our present lives. Jews, African Americans, and indigenous people (among many others) carry their histories in their bodies. We now know family and historical legacies can be passed on unconsciously, through changes in DNA and a baby's experience in the womb. The result: the world may feel constantly dangerous, leaving a child feeling inexplicably frightened, shut down, wary, or despairing.

An unhealthy world.

The world is a troubled place. Injustice. Inequality. Hate. The effects of racism. The specter of climate change. The impact of big and powerful bullies in both government and industry. The result: a heavy burden of hurt and a growing need to defend against the pain to function in everyday life.

How we learn to protect...

Dilemma:

Too much autonomic noise makes it hard to think, function, and go on with daily life.

Solution:

Turn away, and try not to think about it.

It works! (Mostly)

Now it's easier to focus on daily life.

West & Walker, 2018

Attach

Fight

Flight

Freeze

Submit

So now I can function, but I'm not exactly happy.

When patterns of protection grow...

The problem is that avoiding internal chaos by habitually turning away from it tends to create new problems. Powerful feelings of fear, failure, loneliness, rage, and shame cannot be suppressed altogether. What all of those feelings really need is to be listened to, fully gotten, and soothed. If they are not tended to, they eventually show up as flashbacks, panic attacks, depression, relationship difficulties, or chronic illness. In more subtle cases, generational trauma can result in a vague sense of worry, sorrow, or dread. If these patterns are not addressed, life can become terrifying, chronically ruminative, or a flat wasteland. Remember all the symptoms listed on page 7?

So, we need a new strategy...

New Strategy:

Turn toward all parts
without becoming overwhelmed!

Sometimes on our own and sometimes with the help of a therapist, we can learn to turn toward our autonomic defenses, old memories, and painful experiences (humiliations, deprivations, violations)—but this time, because there are now resources for healing those exiled hurting places in us, they can come forward without overwhelming our whole being.

How? We do this by naming and coming to know our symptoms as communications from "parts" of ourselves, which they are! We learn to be curious about them because, believe it or not, all "parts" have been trying to help us the only way they know how.

West & Walker, 2018

"Tracking" or "Mapping" Your Parts

How do we turn toward all parts of ourselves without becoming overwhelmed?

We get to know our symptoms—the "parts" of ourselves we have turned away from—in a new way. "Tracking" or "mapping" parts can help us view them as just parts—not the whole of us. It can help us value their strategies and how they have tried to help, either by offering protection or by hiding our vulnerabilities.

The goal is not to get rid of symptoms, but to understand what they have been trying to do for us. Nor do we want to get rid of parts. Bear in mind, even though every single human alive has parts, those of us with histories of trauma, abuse, and neglect have parts that carry heavy burdens of hurt and shame. They took on those burdens and extreme roles at a time when there was nobody there to help.

There are many creative ways to track/map parts. *These are steps many people find useful.*

1 **Choose a symptom or behavior you're having trouble with—the "part" you want to get to know.**

My controlling part that my kids and partner hate.

2 **Record your inside experience of this part: Thoughts, feelings, and body sensations.**

Thoughts: I'll explode if I don't take action right now.

Feelings: Angry, panicky, terrified, alone

Body sensations: Tightness around my heart, restricted breath, tingling hands and feet

3 Does this part feel like it's in hyper-arousal or hypo-arousal? *(refer to page 9)*

Definitely HYPER-AROUSAL

4 Does it feel like fight, flight, freeze, attach, or submit? Or a combination? *(refer to page 13)*

A combination of FIGHT & ATTACH.

5 What triggers this part?
What causes it to blend with you?

When I'm afraid someone I love is doing something risky. Or when I have the feeling of doom that I have no power at all.

6 What is at risk if this part stopped doing its job?

My loved ones would be in danger. I wouldn't matter. I feel like I would disappear.

7 What might have been really helpful about having a part like this in your childhood?

It helped me feel some power in a situation where almost everything was scary and out of control.

8 How long has this part been trying to help in this way?

As long as I can remember. I know, for sure, since age six.

9 Do you think you need this part in the same way you did when you were at that age, under those circumstances?

Sometimes I do! But, no, not in general. I have a lot of choices I didn't have then.

10 Ask "How old does the part think you are?" (The "you" referred to here is the most wise, centered, grown-up aspect of you.)

I think the part thinks I'm still very young. So it's sort of overprotective.

11 What helps this part to calm even 5%?

- Taking a walk. Listening to music. Calling a safe person. Noticing what is happening in the present moment. The temperature of the air. The texture of the clothes I'm wearing. To notice three things I can hear and three things I can see right now in the present.

- To say "This is just a part of me, not the whole of me."

- To say to the part "I know you're there, and I will come back to you again."

- To ask the part "What do you need from me right now?"

23

Getting to know & care for your parts.

Over time, as you map more and more of your parts, they will begin to like the attention they are receiving and will begin to trust you more. Most importantly, they will begin to understand that they are no longer alone—because they have you!

If you were abused or neglected in childhood, you may not know how to turn toward your parts with compassion. You may relate to them as your parents related to you. This is understandable!

Remember the concept of Self that was introduced a few pages back? Self is your very essence. You're in Self when you feel calm, curious, clear-headed, connected to yourself and others, have an open and compassionate heart, and the courage to face difficult things. Rest assured, you have it too, buried under everything that life piled on top of it. But if you can't fathom how to find it within yourself, a good enough friend, partner, or therapist can lend you some of theirs, until it gets easier.

Remember:

- All parts think they are still helping you survive, either physically or psychically, even if some have negative consequences.

- Hyper-aroused parts (fight, flight, attach) are parts that help you mobilize to seek safety.

- Hypo-aroused parts (submit, immobilized freeze) are parts that help you shrink, be less of a threat to an abuser, or less of a target.

- As you learn to relate to parts with increasing Self-energy, they begin to settle down, and you will feel more calm and hopeful in everyday life. This is evidence that your window of tolerance is expanding and that you are making progress, even though there is more work to do.

Parts come in three flavors

Self

Managers

Type A
Executive

Caretaker

Harsh Critic

Firefighters

Compulsive
Drinker

Compulsive
Eater

Compulsive
Exerciser

Exiles

Schwartz, 2001

Terrified
Toddler

Hungry
Baby

Hostile &
Lonely Teen

Confused &
Angry
Kindergartener

Ashamed
Preteen

Neglected
Infant

Getting to know
Protectors

There are two types of protectors: Managers & Firefighters

Managers are proactive. They say, "Never again will I be caught off guard!" They plan, control, strive, criticize, worry, and care for others. They help us get on with daily life, while doing everything they can to avoid vulnerable feelings.

Most people like their managers a great deal because they get things done, they look good to others, and they often get lots of approval from the outside world for achievements, high standards, and caretaking of others. All their hard work often leaves them exhausted, but you can still take credit for the resourcefulness your managers employ to keep your life running smoothly.

Schwartz, 2001

Managers

Harsh Critic　　　Type A Executive

Caretaker　　　Burdened People-Pleaser

Firefighters

Firefighters are reactive. They put out emotional fires when managers fail to keep the flames tamped down. They have to act fast. They are impulsive, desperate, and even destructive. They can also be heroic and fearless. This is the realm of addictions and compulsions.

Often people don't care for their firefighters because even though they are working hard to protect vulnerable parts of the personality, they can have messy and unpleasant consequences. They are extreme, by definition. Their function is to either distract or dissociate until the flames are quelled. Examples of common firefighters are a compulsive eater, shopper, or gambler; one who self-harms; one who dissociates or goes into fantasy; or one who makes us sick, chronically sleepy/exhausted, or even suicidal.

At first, these parts are hard to like! And we usually get a lot of grief from others about our firefighters' strategies! But they may have saved our lives when we were being abused or neglected or when we suffered an unbearable trauma. They learned to turn on the fire hose, full blast.

The Hero

Lost in Fantasy

Compulsive Exerciser

Compulsive Shopper

Getting to know Exiles

Exiles are the vulnerable parts of the personality. Often young and scared, they carry shame, rage, terror, grief, loneliness, and dependency. They carry the memories of childhood abuse and neglect, as well as the toxic beliefs that often get stored with the pain—like "I don't matter" or "I'm worthless." In the past, in order to get on with daily living, they had to be shut away. Now we can let them know that it is safe to be seen and heard. Now they can be held and loved. This is where the most profound healing happens.

Some people can connect with exiles on their own, but most need a skilled therapist to help them make contact with their exiled child parts. This is because most exiles are scared and in hiding. Often they are surrounded by protective managers and firefighters that make it hard to access them. Once a connection is made, exiles will need to tell their stories fully and then, in good time, release the feelings, beliefs, and body sensations they have been carrying. Releasing this stored pain feels as if a heavy burden has been released—because it has! This unburdening often comes with lots of tears, anger, and powerful body sensations but also a profound awareness that the suffering is over. The result is that exiles can become the delightful children they were meant to be. Often there is a newfound freedom, a sense of healthy entitlement, and the ability to connect with others.

Even though there is no way to rush an exile's healing, the goal of parts therapy is to help exiles release their burdens so they work in harmony with other parts and can offer their playful creativity to the rest of the personality and the world.

Schwartz, 2001

EXILES

Abandoned Infant   Lonely Child   Angry Teenager   Terrified Toddler   Hungry Baby

Inner Critics

One special category of protectors that every trauma survivor seems to have is a relentless inner critic—usually several of them. This is a part that learned to criticize you on the inside, before anyone with more power could do so on the outside. Inner critics can make life a painful slog and can slow your progress in therapy as well, so they are worthy of extra attention.

You might think of inner critics as vulnerable sheep in scary wolves' clothing. They speak with harsh grown-up voices. They try to exert control, intimidate, and undermine. Yet, when you get to know them, they are scared kids themselves, often no older than the vulnerable child parts they protect.

Inner critics come in a lot of different forms. Some want you to conform so you won't risk rejection by standing out. Some impose relentless standards in the hope that you will avoid experiencing shame or being criticized by other people. Others will undermine your self-worth so that you will not take risks and will remain safe by staying small.

One particularly painful critic makes you feel guilty for past wrongs and never lets you off the hook so you won't repeat the same mistakes again. Still others seek to control your every thought and action, as if letting up would risk mediocrity and ultimate failure. But perhaps the most confounding critic of all is the one who seeks to destroy you by questioning your right to exist, as if even being alive is too dangerous. This one, too, thinks it is protecting you.

Working with Inner Critics

The first step in working with an inner critic is to recognize its particular energy and voice and to then cultivate curiosity about how it might be trying to help.

Think: This is a part, though it feels like all of me.

Ask: Why are you blending with me now? What are you worried about right now?

Get curious: What might have been really helpful about having a part like you when I was a kid?

Over time, as you have more conversations with your critical parts, they will be more likely to trust you. Like other protectors in your system, when they feel sufficiently appreciated, they will let you meet the young exiles they protect. By gently witnessing the exile's story, and allowing it to release its burdens, the protector will not feel needed in the same way. Instead, it will be free to rest or to help you in a new way.

Earley & Weiss, 2013

Self

Calm

Creativity

Curiosity

Clarity

Connectedness

Courage

Compassion

Self-Energy

Self-energy exists in everyone. The Self is not a part. You may visualize it as the point of light at your core that was there the moment your life began, and it will always be there—the light that has never been touched by the abuses you have suffered. It cannot be destroyed. But hurt, wounded, and powerful parts can eclipse it, and healing those parts can liberate it.

If you have trouble grasping what Self-energy feels like, think of being with a pet or a person you love. Notice the shift that takes place in your body. Try taking a restorative yoga class. Check in with your mind and body at the beginning of the class and again at the end. Notice the change. Spend some time in nature. Cultivate an open awareness of the beauty around you. Notice the shift that takes place in your body. Listen to a guided meditation. Take stock of your internal state before and after. Singing, chanting, or moving in a group also uncovers Self-energy for many.

These are just a few suggestions. As you begin to unburden your wounded exiles, your ability to rest in Self-energy will grow, and your life and relationships will transform.

Silver Linings

Just as the world is beautiful and broken, we too are beautiful and broken. Personal freedom depends upon embracing it *all*, one day at a time. Huge emotions. Flashbacks and triggering memories. Unhelpful habitual patterns in relationships. The grief that recovery and healing is such a long process. And especially, healing requires that we embrace all our parts. Their pace. Their pain. Like a warm and generous grandparent, spread your arms wide to embrace all your scared and vulnerable inner children, waiting to tell their stories. Tuck them under your wings like a hen with her new chicks.

This path can lead to surprising and splendid silver linings: deeper empathy for yourself and others than you thought possible, more awe in the most mundane everyday things, more creativity than you dared dream was within reach, and a sweeter reverence for those you love and for those who love you.

What can you do to foster your own recovery?

All Parts Welcome

A daily practice of welcoming…

– Sit quietly at the same time each day.

– Welcome all parts who wish to come to a safe, neutral meeting place.

– Ask: What do you want to let me know about your worries or fears?

– Send the message: You are no longer alone. I am here.

Fisher, 2017; Schwartz 2001

Self

First aid for triggered parts...

If you were abused, chronically ignored, criticized, or neglected over a long period of time, you probably have lots of parts that have extreme feelings and roles. The unpacking should be slow and careful. Likewise, if you suffered a trauma that was so severe that it shifted your fundamental reality—your worldview, your ability to trust, your faith in yourself and others—remember the process of healing will require the utmost care and boundless compassion. Don't rush. Slow is fast. Just as in the practice of yoga, trying to force your muscles into unfamiliar poses too quickly will only cause injury and setbacks, trying to force your parts into health will only cause backlash within your inner family of parts.

When in doubt, cultivate mindfulness and curiosity.

If you have a part that feels a chronic sense of dread, you're not alone. If you have a part that carries the belief that you're not enough or need to work harder, faster, smarter—you are not the only one. These are completely normal parts for survivors of trauma. If you feel overwhelmed at times because your feelings are too intense to tolerate, practice coming back into the present moment with mindful awareness. Lengthen your spine, feel your feet on the floor. Go outside and listen for sounds of nature. Feel the air. Then cultivate curiosity about what part might be asking for attention. The more times you employ mindfulness, curiosity, and compassion toward your parts, the easier it will become, and change will happen.

Fisher, 2017; Schwartz 2001

Notice:	I'm overwhelmed.
Say:	This is a flashback.
Say:	These must be the thoughts, feelings, and emotions of a part.
Notice:	It must be a part, but I don't know which part because it feels like all of me.
Say:	Some part of me is overwhelmed.
Ask:	Who is overwhelmed?
Think:	If I was in my wisest Self, what would I tell myself?
Think:	If someone I love (a niece/nephew, a friend's child) was experiencing this same thing, how would I counsel them?
Ask:	What are three things I see? Really look. What are three things I hear? How close or how far are these sounds? What are three things I smell? What are three textures I can feel right now?
Affirm:	I am safe in the present, *right now*.
Ask:	Is my breathing shallow or nice and deep in my belly? If it's shallow, take three nice deep breaths, with a nice loooong sighing exhale.
Affirm:	I am here breathing in the present, *right now*.
Ask:	What might help my parts feel just a little calmer right now?

About the Author & Illustrator

Colleen West is a Licensed Marriage & Family Therapist, an Internal Family Systems Approved Consultant, an EMDR International Consultant, and has extensive teaching, training, and clinical experience resolving simple and complex trauma. She lives in the San Francisco Bay Area, and divides her time between seeing clients, mentoring clinicians, and writing. She loves the outdoors, writing poetry, and sharing vegetarian feasts with friends and family.

More at colleenwest.com and smarttherapytools.com

Steven is a 2D animator living in Los Angeles. He has worked on the video game Freedom Finger, the animated series Vans Classic Tales, and various shows under Legendary Digital Networks. He likes to fill sketchbooks and take his energetic terrier Charlie to the soccer field at night to play fetch.

More at stevengong.work

References

Anderson, F. G., Sweezy, M., & Schwartz, R. C. (2017). *Internal family systems skills training manual: Trauma-informed treatment for anxiety, depression, PTSD & substance abuse.* PESI Publishing & Media.

Brown, D. P., & Elliot, D. S. (2016). *Attachment disturbances in adults: Treatment for comprehensive repair.* W. W. Norton & Company.

Earley, J., & Weiss, B. (2013). *Freedom from your inner critic: A self-therapy approach.* Sounds True, Inc.

Fisher, J. (2017). *Healing the fragmented selves of trauma survivors: Overcoming internal self-alienation.* Routledge Taylor & Francis Group.

Fisher, J. (2017). *Psychoeducational aids for working with psychological trauma.* Author.

Manfield, P. (2010). *Dyadic resourcing: Creating a foundation for processing trauma.* CreateSpace Independent Publishing.

Manfield, P. (2013). *EMDR up close: Subtleties of trauma processing.* CreateSpace Independent Publishing.

McConnell, S. (2020). *Somatic internal family systems therapy: Awareness, breath, resonance, movement and touch in practice.* North Atlantic Books.

Menakem, R. (2017). *My grandmother's hands: Racialized trauma and the pathway to mending our hearts and bodies.* Central Recovery Press.

Paulsen, S. (2009). *Looking through the eyes of trauma and dissociation: An illustrated guide for EMDR therapists and clients.* Booksurge Publishing.

Paulsen, S. (2017). *When there are no words: Repairing early trauma and neglect from the attachment period with EMDR therapy.* CreateSpace Independent Publishing.

Schwartz, J., & Brennan, B. (2013). *There's a part of me…* Trailheads Publications.

Schwartz, R. C. (2008). *You are the one you've been waiting for: Bringing courageous love to intimate relationships.* Trailheads Publications.

Schwartz, R. C., & Sweezy, M. (2020). *Internal family systems therapy* (2nd ed.). Guilford Press.

Shapiro, F. (1995). *Eye movement desensitization and reprocessing: Basic principles, protocols, and procedures.* Guilford Press.

Steele, K., Boon, S., & van der Hart, O. (2017). *Treating trauma-related dissociation: A practical, integrative approach.* W. W. Norton & Company.

van der Hart, O., Nijenhuis, E. R. S., & Steele, K. (2006). *The haunted self: Structural dissociation and the treatment of chronic traumatization.* W. W. Norton & Company.

van der Kolk, B. (2014). *The body keeps the score: Brain, mind, and body in the healing of trauma.* Penguin Books.

Walker, P. (2013). *Complex PTSD: From surviving to thriving.* Azure Coyote Publishing.

West, C., & Walker, R. (2018). *Understanding trauma: A survivor's guide.* Author. Berkeley, CA.